MADELINE NINA MUNRO was born in England and served as a physical education instructor with the ATS during World War II. In 1945 she came to New Zealand and qualified as a homecraft teacher at Christchurch Teachers' Training College. In 1964 she married Jim Munro and came to Napier, where she is director of a small company importing handicrafts from the developing countries. Her recreations include experimental cookery, herb cultivation, and batik and fabric printing.

JAMES STUART BURNETT MUNRO was born in Scotland and was engaged in public works engineering in that country and, for seven years, in Iran. He came to New Zealand and joined the Ministry of Works but was later appointed Director of the Hawke's Bay Art Gallery and Museum, in which post he has been working for the past sixteen years. His hobbies include "gardening, cooking, beer and winemaking, swimming, and snoozing in the sun".

A TASTE OF
NEW ZEALAND
IN FOOD AND PICTURES

NINA and JIM MUNRO

A.H. & A.W. REED LTD
Wellington Sydney London

For All the Children

First published 1977
Reprinted 1978

A.H. & A.W. REED LTD
65-67 Taranaki Street, Wellington
53 Myoora Road, Terrey Hills, Sydney 2084
11 Southampton Row, London WC1B 5HA
also
16-18 Beresford Street, Auckland
Cnr Mowbray & Thackeray Streets,
Waltham, Christchurch 2

ISBN 0 589 01078 6

Typesetting by A.H. & A.W. Reed Ltd.
Printed by Kyodo-Shing Loong Pte. Singapore.

ONTENTS

Acknowledgments

We thank the many kind friends who have helped us to compile this book, in particular: Alan Bellamy, Joan Bennett, Ngaire Bradwell, Betty Harris, Kay Mooney, Carol Noble, Frank Robson, Barbara Thompson, and the staff of the Hawke's Bay Art Gallery and Museum. Also, Arnold Wall of Reeds for his help and encouragement.

For permission to reproduce the photographs we thank the Hawke's Bay Art Gallery and Museum, the National Archives, and the Alexander Turnbull Library. We regret that some old photos defied all our efforts to find their source. Individual credits are as follows:

The Hawke's Bay Art Gallery and Museum: the photographs on pages: 5, 19, 25, 27, 59, 60, 63, 70, 79, 82, 88, 95, 99, 101, 105, 110, 117, 118.

National Archives: the photograph on page 3.

National Museum: the photographs on pages 9, 45.

The Alexander Turnbull Library main collection: the photographs on pages, viii, 6, 11, 13, 14, 17, 20, 22, 28, 30, 33, 35, 36, 38, 41, 42, 47, 49, 51, 53, 54, 57, 65, 66, 68, 73, 74, 77, 80, 85, 87, 91, 93, 96, 102, 107, 109, 112, 115.

The following collections housed in the Alexander Turnbull Library: the Berry Collection: 35; the Cameron Collection: viii, 42, 107; the Godber Collection: 33, 66; the Guest Collection: 102; the Head Collection: 80; the Jones Collection 20, 41, 51, 73, 74, 93; the McAllister Collection: 11, 65; the Making New Zealand Collection: 13, 38, 53; the Northwood Collection: 14, 36, 57, 112; the Price Collection: 28, 87; the Steffano Webb Collection: 17; the Tesla Collection: 30, 85; the Wall Collection: 96.

N. and J.M.

INTRODUCTION

AS NEW SETTLERS of nearly thirty years ago we can still remember the surprise and delight with which we tasted and enjoyed some of the typically New Zealand recipes, fruits and vegetables, new to us who had been brought up in the northern hemisphere. But on looking around today we discover that the new generation has little or no knowledge of many of the typical dishes that we so enjoyed; and persuaded by many enquiries on how to do this and that, we decided we would attempt to bring up to date some of the recipes which have stood the test of time.

Basically the background of New Zealand cooking is the country cooking of England, Scotland, Ireland and Wales, with some overtones of the various European settlers who have settled here in the last 100 years.

Lots of recipes we have never met anywhere else, as the original British recipe was adapted using the ingredients available locally. The New Zealand woman prided herself on her ability to produce lavish spreads for the main social occasions in the early days. The old cookery books are full of biscuit, scone and cake recipes of all varieties, each trying to be a little different.

The recipes range from those using subtropical fruits grown in the far north to those suitable for a colder climate in the South Island where a lot of Scottish recipes are still used almost unchanged.

We have also included some Maori recipes. There are no doubt many favourite New Zealand recipes we have left out but this, after all, is only a "Taste" of New Zealand.

Nina and Jim Munro

Recipe For a Social Evening

Secure an equal number of young men and maidens. In choosing the former avoid any that look at all green or soft, and in the case of the latter choose those that look sweet and fresh, carefully avoiding any that have at all a sour appearance. Place near a good fire, but not too near, as it is apt to spoil the dressing. Flavour with club chat, into which something rather spicy has been thrown. If any part of the dish is seen to be growing over-tender a little re-mixing is advisable. This danger sometimes arises through two spoons being in the dish. Leave to simmer until it begins to sing. Then, when it is looking rather done, the ingredients may be removed and well stuffed, a little spirit being dropped into each, but care must be taken not to overdo the latter, as it may foam and clash with the other ingredients. The dish must now be carefully watched and the moment all the spirit has evaporated it should be well covered up and packed away.

Tennis spectators, 1890

PIKELETS

In most British cookery books pikelets are described as a miniature form of crumpet–unsweetened and having yeast as their rising agent. The New Zealand version is sweeter, blander and softer, much more quickly prepared and cooked.

The name is derived from Welsh bara pyglyd, *and the pikelet may have been brought to New Zealand by Welsh miners migrating to the goldfields. In its present form it was being served at afternoon teas and at picnics in the 1880s, and possibly much earlier than that.*

220 g (8 oz) plain flour
2 tablespoons sugar
1 teaspoon bicarbonate of soda
1½ teaspoons cream of tartar
pinch of salt
2 eggs beaten with enough milk to make 280 ml (½ pint) liquid

Sift all the dry ingredients together, then beat in the egg mixture, beating well to include as much air as possible. If time allows, let batter stand for 3—4 hours then beat well again.

Drop dessertspoonfuls of mixture on to a hot greased griddle iron, or electric plate. When bubbles appear, turn over. Should be light brown on both sides.

Serve hot or cold with jam and whipped cream, or buttered.

The tennis players opposite are eating something unfamiliar to a modern tennis court–possible outsize pikelets. The game is being played in early spring, for the creeper on the fence is only just coming into leaf; and the day is a little chilly, for feather boas are in evidence, and there is a rug over the knees.

1

BARLEY BROTH

1 kg (2 lb) neck of mutton trimmed of fat
90 g (3 oz) pearl barley
90 g (3 oz) dried peas, or fresh if obtainable
1 large onion, sliced
white of one leek
1 small cabbage
3 carrots, diced
2 white turnips
2 tablespoons chopped parsley
2.5 l (5 pints) of water
salt and pepper

Put the meat into a large saucepan with the water, bring to the boil and then skim the top. (If using dried peas add them with the meat to begin with.) Season to taste and simmer gently for about 1 hour.

Now add the root vegetables and barley and cook covered for another 20 minutes. Five minutes before serving add shredded cabbage and parsley.

Serve one cutlet per person, adjusting seasoning.
Vegetables can be varied according to the season.

(Serves 6–8)

New Zealand was one of the first countries to introduce State pensions for the aged—this was in 1898. Up to that time the citizen was expected to be thrifty, to make provision for his or her old age.

To help and encourage saving there were many "friendly societies" to which a worker could contribute a part of his wages and which would give him some support in sickness or old age; also the churches and sundry charitable organisations did what they could for those fallen on hard days.

Some cities had a mayoral coal-and-blanket fund to provide some warmth in winter; and country people have always been neighbourly to the unfortunate of their district.

Even so, the inevitable loneliness of old age was too often accompanied by near-starvation, the absence of medical care, and by cold and discomfort in the home.

In such houses housekeeping had to be frugal. Mutton, particularly before it began to be refrigerated and exported, was the cheapest of butchers' meats, and every housewife worthy of the name had an extensive repertoire of mutton dishes to choose from.

The old lady in the photograph is smoking a pipe—no great rarity, this, in Victorian times. Samuel Butler, author of Erewhon, *writing of an old lady seen in Christchurch in the 1860s says, "I saw her standing near the market . . . her petticoat was of dark green and the upper part of her dress was scarlet—a kerchief was folded not ungracefully about her head and she was smoking a short black cutty pipe—splendidly coloured."*

Pensioners at home

FARMHOUSE RABBIT

In the late twentieth century rabbit has become a rare delicacy in New Zealand. It may not legally be offered for sale, and the only way in which the city-dweller can get hold of one now is through the kindness of country friends—but even so, in most country areas the rabbit has been almost exterminated.

Introduced between 1840 and 1860, by the 1880s the rabbit had become a pest of terrible destructiveness, particularly in the lower-rainfall provinces. It was bankrupting farmers, and whole stations had to be abandoned to it—while some made moderate fortunes from the export of skins and frozen carcasses.

In the words of a New Zealand poet:

> Where the sheep feed there feed I,
> Depleted lands behind me lie,
> Of dogs and guns I take no heed,
> I only breed and breed and breed.

Not until 1952 was the problem tackled on a national scale. One of the first steps of the Rabbit Destruction Council then formed was to prohibit the sale of rabbits; it became worth nobody's effort to cash in on the skin and meat.

Within twenty-five years Bunny was under control: whereas in the 1940s the country roads were strewn with the dead bodies of rabbits run over at night, today one may drive many hundreds of kilometres and see no rabbits at all.

But the New Zealand gourmet mourns their passing. In Christchurch in the 1920s, a good fat rabbit, skin and all, would retail for threepence: and you could buy a stuffed and roasted rabbit for one shilling. Excellent fare for a golfer's lunch.

1 rabbit
5 large onions
2 slices stale white bread
1 tablespoon fresh sage, chopped
1 teaspoon fresh thyme, chopped
1 lemon rind, grated
salt and pepper, and a piece of butter

Joint the rabbit, soak in salted water while making the stuffing.
Chop onion roughly, cover with water in saucepan and bring to boil. Strain off water.
Soak two thick slices of stale bread in a little water and squeeze dry.
Mix bread, grated lemon rind, onions, herbs, salt and pepper and piece of butter together well.
Grease a baking tin well, take rabbit joints out of the water, shake but do not dry them.
Spread stuffing all over each joint.
Put into tin and cover with baking foil, pressing it down well to keep the steam in.
Cook for 2 hours at 450°F/232°C, remove foil after first hour so that the stuffing can get crisp and brown.
Serve with boiled potatoes and carrots.

On the way to the tee

Wellington tramcar

COTTAGE CHEESE

"Slowly and steadily the car came down the track from the Newtown shed, brilliantly lighted inside with eight 16-candlepower lamps, having a 32-candlepower headlight, and the destination lights (showing the words Wellington to Newtown *at each end) were of 16-candlepower. Besides this lighting, frequent flashes of electricity were thrown off by the works beneath the car, and the point of contact of the connecting arm with the trolley-wire overhead showed a vivid blue light. The whole spectacle as the car proceeded along the track was unique and brilliant." So wrote a local reporter on 8 June 1904 of the trial trip at midnight of Wellington's first tramcar.*

Sixty years later Wellington's and New Zealand's last tram, amid scenes of great emotion, made her last trip—Thorndon to Newtown, but Wellingtonians may still enjoy a nostalgic tramride over a short length of track at Queen Elizabeth II Park at Paekakariki.

But slow, noisy and grimy they were. And, squeezed to suffocation-point during the rush hours.

Squeezing is an essential part of the ritual of home cheesemaking. In the old days every self-respecting farm ran a house-cow that kept the family in milk and cream; the farmer's wife made her own butter and cheese, and any surplus milk and buttermilk were fed to the pigs.

The cottage cheese described opposite is simple to make and delicious to eat.

1 l (2 pints) of milk
1 tablespoon plain rennet
¼ teaspoon salt

Warm milk to blood heat, then pour into mixing bowl and add rennet and salt. Leave to set.
Then pour into sieve lined with a piece of muslin or an old piece of sheet, leave overnight to drain.
Then put a weight on top to squeeze out surplus moisture (about 30 minutes), then mash with fork, adding more salt to taste and some chopped chives or other herbs if desired.
Keeps well in pots in the fridge.
Can be used plain for cooking or making cheesecake.

CREAM CHEESE:

As above but cream is used instead of milk. This gives a richer, smoother cheese.

CRAYFISH, MARINE AND FRESHWATER (KOURA)

The New Zealand marine crayfish (Jasus edwardsii) *is often described as "lobster" by local hoteliers who ought to know better. There is no New Zealand lobster or* hommard; *the local cray is more akin to the French* langouste. *In Britain the term crayfish applies only to the freshwater species. New Zealand does not use the alternative spelling, crawfish.*

Unhappily for the local gourmet, marine crayfish now command a very high price as they are exported in great quantity to Europe and North America, where unscrupulous restaurants palm them off on their customers as local lobster. Conservationists as well as gourmets deplore this export trade—it is alleged that overfishing may deplete the species to below recovery-point. Compared with lobster, the marine cray has a sweeter flavour and more rubbery texture; also it lacks the large pincers of the lobster, but the flesh of the legs is extremely succulent.

Crayfish may be served up as in any of the classic lobster recipes, but purists hold that the best recipe of all is the one given below.

The smaller freshwater koura are plentiful in lakes and rivers, but few people—except the Maori, who knows a good thing when he eats it—will take the trouble to catch them. Those who have eaten the French écrevisse *will enjoy koura.*

CRAYFISH:

If possible procure the fish alive. Put into saucepan of boiling salted water. But if you cannot bear the thought of doing this or the thrashing that occurs, put the crayfish in a pan of cold fresh water and bring very slowly to the boil, adding one dessertspoon of salt when boiling. Cook 20—30 minutes according to size. Rub shell over with a little butter. Take the body from the tail. Divide tail, head and body into halves. Take off large claws and crack at joints. Arrange on platter and decorate with parsley.

The *koura*, or freshwater crayfish, is common in most of our lakes and streams. It can grow to 250 mm (10 in.) in length but the average size is half this. The flesh is sweeter than that of the saltwater crayfish. It is cooked in the same manner as the marine crayfish and usually the tail only is eaten.

Artist at Lake Taupo

HOMELY REMEDIES

The waiting-room is that of an expensively fashionable city doctor: the patients of humbler practitioners made do with benches or hardwood chairs.

If we judge the health of our forefathers by the press advertisements of the day they suffered many ailments. To list only a few—abscesses, acidity, acne, adenoids, adiposity, alcoholism, alopecia, anaemia, astigmatism, baldness, barber's itch, biliousness, bladder troubles, boils, Bright's disease, bronchitis, bunions, carbuncles, catarrh, chilblains, chlorosis, cholera, colic, constipation, consumption, coughs, croup, dandruff, deafness, debility, dermatitis, diarrhoea, dropsy, dysentery—the tally goes on and on. . . .

Doctors and dentists were relatively few in number, and their knowledge was limited. The well-to-do citizen ate and drank prodigiously, the very poor were close to starvation: the health of both was bound to suffer accordingly.

The housewife had to have some knowledge of nursing and first aid, for the doctor might live many miles away. He could not be summoned or consulted by telephone and must travel slowly on his horse or in his gig: as a result, the newspapers carried home-health columns, the booksellers found family-doctor manuals could be bestsellers, and cookery books usually included a chapter or two on domestic medicines, nursing and first aid, and elementary cosmetics.

A SPICE POULTICE

5 teaspoons each of:
   cinnamon; allspice; cloves; aniseed

The whole seeds are slightly bruised and quilted between two layers of flannel, and the poultice is ready for use.
When required it must be dipped into hot water, sprinkled with surgical spirit and applied to the abdomen of the sufferer.
It gives great relief to children who are suffering from griping pains, and should be available in every nursery.

   from *Tetaka Kai*—published by the Napier Rowing Club, 1906.

TO REMOVE A SPLINTER
Nearly fill a widemouthed bottle with hot water.
Hold the injured part over this, and press down tightly.
The suction will act as a poultice and draw the flesh down, when the splinter will come out quite easily.

Doctor's waiting-room

BEEF TEA

Lord Lyttelton and Mr Selfe, 1868

Beef tea as a tonic was known in ancient Rome. Louis XV of France took a mid-morning cup of it made, it was alleged, from no less than four kilos of choicest steak.

The chess-players in the photograph would have believed implicitly in its restorative virtues: was it not obvious that by some process of osmosis the strength of the ox was transferred into the human frame?

But by the 1860s doubts were creeping in. No less an authority than Miss Florence Nightingale had said: "One of the most common errors among nurses, with respect to sick diet, is the belief that beef tea is the most nutritive of all articles. Just try and boil down a pound of beef into beef tea; evaporate your beef tea and see what is left of your beef; you will find that there is barely a teaspoonful of solid nourishment to half a pint of water in beef tea. Nevertheless, there is a certain reparative quality in it—we do not know what—as there is in tea. It may safely be given in almost any inflammatory disease but is little to be depended upon with the healthy or convalescent, where much nourishment is required."

But, as the date of the opposite recipe shows, beef tea was still popular enough to merit a mention in 1906, and Constance Spry and Good Housekeeping *in the 1960s were still giving the formula.*

Made as specified here, this classic beverage is clear and refreshing. Commercial bouillon cubes and instant beef stocks are an unworthy and unsatisfactory substitute.

450 g (1 lb) lean beef
570 ml (1 pint) of cold water

Mince the beef finely, and pour over it the cold water, stir and allow to stand for 1 hour.

Place basin covered in saucepan of water and gently boil for 1 hour.

Pour the cooked beef on to a fine strainer.

The beef tea which runs through contains a quantity of fine sediment which is drunk with the liquid after being slightly salted.

from *Tetaka Kai*—published by the Napier Rowing Club, 1906.

14 *Splitting limestone, Kaitaia*

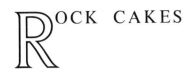

ROCK CAKES

Their name has puzzled more than one student of New Zealand's gastronomic history for, though their texture is short, by no stretch of the imagination can it be considered rocky.

The following recipe gives the explanation and is borne out by Mrs Beeton (1861), who mentions not Rock Cakes but Rock Biscuits, including the advice: "Put the dough, with a fork, on the tins, making it look as rough as possible."

Rock cakes are a staple standby for cakes needed in a hurry, being quick and simple to prepare and cook, and economical in cost. With scones they are a popular teatime ration for shearers, harvesters and musterers.

225 g (8 oz) flour
½ teaspoon baking powder
60 g (2 oz) lard
60 g (2 oz) butter
120 g (4 oz) sugar
90 g (3 oz) currants or sultanas
30 g (1 oz) chopped peel (or marmalade)
pinch salt
1 large egg

Sift flour and salt into mixing bowl, rub in fat until like fine breadcrumbs.
Add sugar, currants and mixed peel.
Beat the egg and gradually blend into dry ingredients with fork until mixture is stiff and rocky.
It must be stiff or it will lose shape when baking.
Put little heaps on greased baking sheet, and bake in centre of 425°F/220°C oven for 15 minutes.
Cool on wire rack.

CLARET CUP

1 bottle of claret or other dry red wine
5 tablespoons of curaçao
2 tablespoons each of brandy and rum
2 large bottles of lemonade
2 large bottles of sodawater
4 tablespoons sugar
grated rind of one small lemon
some ice
spray of borage

Mix all ingredients together well.
Stand in ice for 15—20 minutes before serving.

A party beverage served in Victorian/Edwardian days, usually from a punchbowl. Slightly sweet, gaily coloured, festively fizzy, it was made innocuously weak for teenage dancers, for many of whom it would be their first acquaintance with the Demon Alcohol. They could swig it by the tumbler and be none the worse for it.

The recipe given here is a fraction more potent: more suitable for an adult party where thirsts must be slaked, not drowned. Instances are recorded of irresponsible youths surreptitiously spiking the innocent brew with gin, whose taste is hard to detect. Unseemly disorder was apt to follow, followed by recriminations and some detective work to identify the culprit. If discovered, he was in dire disgrace and a social outcast.

The celebration in the photograph is a modest affair. The gentlemen are in suits, not the morning dress de rigueur *for a fashionable wedding, and the drink is claret or burgundy rather than champagne.*

16

COLONIAL GOOSE

The word mutton, like beef, veal and pork, commemorates the Norman conquest of England in 1066. The Anglo-Saxon serfs used the name of the live animal when cooking for themselves, but their Norman overlords called the cooked meat by the French name, and the distinction has persisted to this day.

New Zealand makes a further distinction: the Scots term hogget is used to describe the animal (and its meat) that is at the two-tooth age—larger, darker and more flavoured than lamb, less mature than mutton.

New Zealanders are sheepfarmers and mutton-cookers par excellence, their history has seen to that. On many farms mutton was the staple meat diet—the day started with chops for break-fast—and the cook had to cudgel her brains to devise means of making mutton diets less drearily monotonous. Colonial Goose is only one of numerous recipes centred on mutton and it is still a favourite in modern household kitchens.

The right wine to accompany lamb, hogget or mutton? European traditionalists may agree that as these are "dark" meats the wine should be a dry red or at least a rosé. New Zealanders are ruggedly independent of such doctrine and will drink any liquid with their mutton—tea, beer or fizzy lemonade. The more discriminating citizen may recommend one of the local dry red wines which, at their best, can startle even a Frenchman by their potability.

leg of mutton, boned
90 g (3 oz) fresh breadcrumbs
90 g (3 oz) finely diced bacon
1 large onion, finely chopped
chopped parsley
1 teaspoon mixed herbs (thyme, sage, majoram)
½ teaspoon grated nutmeg
½ teaspoon grated lemon peel
1 beaten egg
salt and pepper, milk

Mix all dry ingredients together.
Add the egg and just enough milk to moisten, stuff the opening in the meat and tie securely.
Roast in a medium oven 325°F/160°C, allowing 15–20 minutes to each 450 g (1 lb), depending on how well done you like it.
Serve (removing string) with baby boiled or baked potatoes.
Serve gravy separately.

Dipping sheep

ANZAC BISCUITS

The name is a souvenir of World War I, when the Australian-New Zealand forces participating in the ill-fated attack on the Gallipoli peninsula were designated the Australian-New Zealand Army Corps (ANZAC).

At home, the war sparked off the usual series of patriotic follies. Spy-mania was endemic – a German seaplane was positively seen to swoop over the tiny township of Havelock in the Marlborough Sounds. Inoffensive citizens with Germanic surnames hastily anglicised them. The music of Wagner and Beethoven was verboten. German sausage became Belgian sausage overnight.

Patriotism also took more practical forms. Red Cross and other charitable organisations needed funds, and the population reacted with enthusiasm. Among the most favoured ways of money-raising were the "Queen Carnivals" – coin-collecting enterprises that usually culminated in a grand procession of decorated floats which included some less serious ones – as pictured here.

180 g (6 oz) rolled oats
180 g (6 oz) plain flour
180 g (6 oz) desiccated coconut
180 g (6 oz) brown sugar
1½ teaspoons baking powder
200 g (7 oz) butter
2 tablespoons golden syrup

Melt butter with syrup, and pour into all dry ingredients. Mix well.
Shape into balls and flatten with fork.
Bake on greased oven sheet for 15 to 20 minutes in 300°F/150°C oven.

Patriotic procession, Nelson

Chemist's shop, Rotorua

MORE HOME REMEDIES

Happy the little town that grew to the size where it could support a fulltime chemist's shop, for the chemist was not merely a pharmacist, he would also render medical aid in emergency and his shop was an unofficial consulting-room and first-aid post. (The owners of the shop illustrated did not have quite such responsibility, for a card in the window announces that the doctor "attends daily".)

The chemist had competition to contend with, as some doctors conducted their own dispensaries. More importantly, the grocer would have more than one shelf devoted to a battery of patent medicines—antiseptics, balms and balsams, cachets, carminatives, compounds, deodorants, digestants, elixirs, embrocations, emulsions, expectorants, febrifuges, gargles, inhalants, laxatives, liniments, lotions, ointments, painkillers, powders, and assorted salts.

The chemist rolled the pills and concocted the mixtures prescribed by the doctor, sold surgical appliances and nursing requirements and, if he were a shrewd man of business, marketed his own private formulae in competition with the patent-medicine manufacturers. Two or three enterprising chemists made comfortable fortunes in this way.

As mentioned on an earlier page, the housewife was her own pharmacist if need be, and a well-stocked medicine cupboard could be as proud a possession as a well-stocked pantry.

ONE-NIGHT COLD CURE

A Chest or Head Cold can be cured in one night if treated in time. Put on a flannel night dress, and also wrap a blanket well over that; then sit for 15 minutes with the feet and ankles in a mustard and water foot bath as hot as it can be borne, adding more hot water if necessary. Meantime sip a pint of hot strong home-made lemonade (or a glass of hot whisky).

Next dry the feet quickly and get into bed instantly.

Keep the blanket still wrapped around you, as the touch of cold sheets would undo all the work.

The cold will be gone in the morning.

from *Secret Recipes Compiled by an Incapacitated Returned Soldier*, published Clark & Matheson, Auckland, 1927

HOMEMADE HEALTH SALTS

60 g (2 oz) cream of tartar
60 g (2 oz) tartaric acid
60 g (2 oz) epsom salts
60 g (2 oz) magnesia
60 g (2 oz) bicarbonate of soda
10 g (¼ oz) icing sugar

Roll all together and mix thoroughly. Store in airtight bottle.

VICTORIA SPONGE CAKE

Loyal subjects of the Great White Queen
scattered her name all over New Zealand.
Streets, squares, monuments, a waterfall, public houses
still bear it; a brand of men's braces and countless tearooms
were proud of it in their time. And the sponge cake endureth. . . .

120 g (4 oz) butter, softened
120 g (4 oz) sugar
2 eggs
120 (4 oz) plain flour
1 teaspoon baking powder

Line the bottoms of two 200 mm (7 in.) sandwich tins and grease the sides well. Preheat the oven to 335°F/175°C.

Cream the butter and sugar, add the eggs and then sift in the dry ingredients. Beat them together with a wooden spoon for 2 or 3 minutes until they are smooth.

Divide equally between the two tins, smoothing the tops with a palette knife. Bake in the middle of the oven for 25 to 35 minutes, cool on a wire rack.

Spread cream and sliced strawberries in the middle, and dust with icing sugar.

You can add coffee, walnuts, grated orange rind or lemon peel to vary the recipe.

Victorian fireplace

BAKED SWAN

The gentlemen in the photograph are not a flying squad of police-men but members of an early cycling club wearing one of the elaborate club uniforms of the early days. The mounts include a velocipede or "boneshaker", the forerunner of the penny-farthing cycles also seen in this picture.

The swan of the recipe is usually the Australian black swan (Cygnus atratus), *an introduced species that has acclimatised satisfactorily.*

White swan were jealously preserved as a royal dish in England from Norman times onward, one of the City of London livery companies—the Vintners—having enjoyed the privilege since 1509 of holding an annual Swan Feast in return for marking, or "upping", the Thames swans every year on the sovereign's behalf. The Feast is still held but cygnets, not adult birds, are served up.

STUFFING

360 g (12 oz) finely chopped onion
450 g (1 lb) breadcrumbs
1 teaspoon chopped thyme
1 dessertspoon finely chopped sage
1 beaten egg
30 g (1 oz) melted butter

Soak breadcrumbs for few minutes in warm water, then squeeze dry. Mix with onion, sage, thyme and seasoning. Add beaten egg and melted butter. Stuff bird and sew up opening.

Put stuffed swan in large pot quarter-filled with boiling water and simmer for 2 hours.

Take out of pot and flour well. Put into baking dish with a little dripping or butter and bake for 1 hour in moderate oven 350°F/ 180°C until nicely brown.

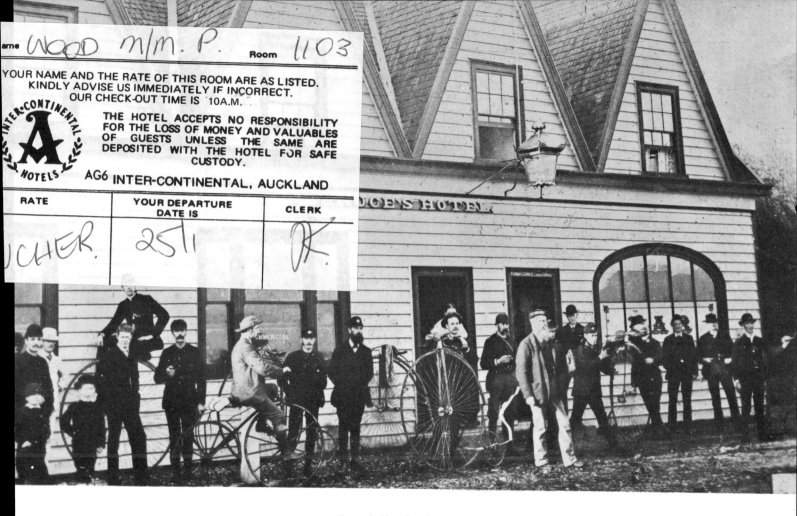

Bruce's Hotel, Ahaura

PAUA SOUP

To prepare paua, scrub under running water to remove sand and black colouring. Remove head and egg, cut off rind. Place in cloth or polythene bag and pound with heavy instrument to tenderise. Slice or mince as required.

This handsome mollusc grows up to fifteen centimetres in length and is common in New Zealand waters. The interior of the shell is highly iridescent and has been much used for ornament by both the ancient Maori and the Pakeha.

The Maori also prized the paua as a comestible but, curiously, few Pakeha ever tasted it until in recent years, possibly because it demanded the special preparation here described. Nowadays it is sometimes on sale in the fish-shops.

PAUA FRITTERS   (serves 4)

240 g (½ lb) paua, minced
120 g (4 oz) flour
2 teaspoons baking powder
½ teaspoon salt
120 ml (4 fluid oz) milk
1 egg, separated

Sift dry ingredients, combine egg yolk with milk, add gradually to dry ingredients.
Fold in stiffly beaten egg white.
Add minced paua.
Fry in oil in tablespoonful lots, both sides.

PAUA SOUP   (serves 6)

700 g (1½ lb) paua, minced
1 l (2 pints) milk
½ teaspoon salt
pepper to taste
2 tablespoons flour

Prepare paua as above. Boil with one half of the milk for 30 minutes, strain.
Mix the flour with some of the other half of the milk then add the rest and heat slowly until it thickens.
Season and serve sprinkled with chopped parsley or chives.

Bathing belles, 1910

"Mr Morton's catch"

ROAST WILD DUCK

History cannot tell us who the Mr Morton of the photograph was but he has had a surprisingly satisfying day, his catch including a red-deer stag, a hare, a large eel, rabbits, and sundry waterfowl. The most common New Zealand native species is the grey duck (Anas superciliosa); *introduced species include mallard, shoveller and teal.*

The ancient Maori used consummate patience in stalking duck feeding on the water, approaching them very slowly with only the hunter's head, camouflaged with floating weed, above water. Then a quick grab and the duck was his. The open duckshooting season is short in comparison with the northern countries' seasons. Modern shooters usually wait for the dawn or evening flight, concealed in a hide or maimai.

1 wild duck
1 onion, chopped finely
180 g (6 oz) stale breadcrumbs
3 teaspoons mixed herbs
60 g (2 oz) butter
salt and pepper

Well pluck, singe and clean the duck.

Mix dry ingredients and rub in butter until crumbly.

Then stuff the duck and sew up opening with string or fasten with small skewer.

Steam in saucepan with two cups of water until tender, then brown in hot oven.

Serve with baked potatoes, kumara and green peas.

Another stuffing may be made with cooking apples peeled and chopped together with some prunes which have been soaked and stoned, seasoned with salt and pepper.

MAORI BREAD   Old Style

"There's nothing to it," said Arch. "anyone can use a camp oven."
"Can you?" I asked.
"Of course. I'll give you one lesson and you'll be away."

I watched him build up a big fire and, when it was reduced to glowing embers, carefully rake it all out. He stood the oven on its three stubby legs on the hot hearth. He popped the already-risen dough into the oven in four pieces, placed the raised lid in position, shovelled red embers on top, and a layer of ashes over the embers.

"Now," he said, "we just forget about it till we think the bread is done."

Some time later he scraped off the ashes and cinders and lifted the lid.

A delicious aroma of freshly-baked bread wafted around the hut and he lifted out the brownest, crispest loaves imaginable. It was simple! Anyone could do it!

from *Beyond the Skippers Road* by Terri Macnicol. Reed, Wellington, 1965

Leaven:
   3 tablespoons flour
   2 tablespoons sugar
   280 ml (½ pint) warm water

Mix the ingredients to a paste and seal in an airtight jar. Stand for 48 hours in a warm place until the mixture has fermented. Then mix:
   2 tablespoons flour
   2 tablespoons sugar
   570 ml (1 pint) of lukewarm water

Add this to the first mixture and leave to stand for another 48 hours. It is then ready for use. Use this leaven as yeast.

Bread:

   680 g (1½ lb) flour
   60 g (2 oz) sugar
   570 ml (1 pint) leaven mixture

Mix all the ingredients well and leave to prove for 8 hours in covered bowl. Then knead mixture thoroughly; more flour may be needed to make a firm dough. Put into camp oven with lid, or into loaf tins, and let rise again for 1½ hours. Bake in a 450°F/230°C for 45–50 minutes.

Slices of potato, kumara or yam, cooked in unsalted water, cooled and mashed, were added to the first stage of leaven in many of the recipes for Maori bread.

When bread was baked every other day, a portion of the unbaked dough was kept back, put into a jar and fed with ½ teaspoon sugar one day and ½ cup of unsalted potato water the next, and was added to hasten the working of the original leaven.

(As published in the *Otago Daily Times,* April 1969)

Baking Bread, Piha

FLUMMERY

1 tablespoon plain white flour
1½ tablespoons of powdered gelatine
120 g (4 oz) sugar
4 oranges (juice only)
1 lemon (juice only)
1 passionfruit (pulp)
whipped cream

With a little cold water mix the flour to a paste, then add one cup of hot water, stirring well.
Put into saucepan and boil 1 minute.
Then add gelatine which has been soaked in ¼ cup of cold water until dissolved.
Then add the sugar, and fruit juices and bring to the boil, stirring all the time.
Pour into bowl and when cool beat until thick and fluffy.
Put into serving bowl and leave for 12 hours in the fridge.
Serve with passionfruit pulp on top, and whipped cream.

Most people born in New Zealand since the year 1907 owe something of their health and vitality to Taranaki-born Sir Frederic Truby King (1858–1938). A medical man of many gifts and a born innovator, he did valuable pioneer work in the fields of plant and livestock nutrition, psychological medicine, soil-erosion control, plant acclimatisation and medical jurisprudence.

But it was in the matter of child welfare that he earned an international reputation. In 1907 he founded the Royal New Zealand Society for the Health of Women and Children (more commonly recognised nowadays as the Plunket Society, named after the wife of Lord Plunket, Governor of New Zealand 1904–10), and so successful was the Society's work under his inspiration and guidance that infant mortality in this country had dropped from 88.8 to 30.9 per 1000 childbirths between 1907 and 1938.

Silver-spoon baby

Transporting milk, around the turn of the century

BROWN BREAD ICE

Until men learned how to manufacture ice they had to make do with winter's supply of the natural article, cutting large blocks of it from frozen ponds and storing it in stone-lined underground ice-houses for summer use. So stored, it would last a surprisingly long time—well into the following autumn.

The invention of ices is attributed to Catherine de Medici (1519–89), and ice-cream recipes were written by the great French chef Marie-Antoine Careme (1784–1833), but the labour and time involved in making ice-cream were formidable. A large outer bowl was filled with crushed ice and saltpetre, an inner bowl containing the mixture was nestled inside it and moved and stirred until the somewhat mushy ice-cream had set; later models were built on the lines of a hand churn, a doggedly patient scullerymaid slowly rotating the handle.

Until manmade refrigeration came to the rescue, natural ice must have been virtually unprocurable in the North Island unless one lived close to the mountains; ice-cream was probably never made in New Zealand until refrigerated meat stores could market block ice as a byproduct of their storage function.

Ices were certainly being sold in tearooms and the curiously named "soda fountains" during World War I, and in Christchurch at least two or three floridly decorated street barrows, tended by picturesque Italians, were dispensing penny ices to the thirsty.

The following recipe describes a teatime treat enjoyed years ago by the boys of Winchester College.

BROWN BREAD ICE
280 ml (½ pint) cream
90 g (3 oz) homemade brown bread
30 g (1 oz) sugar
3 tablespoons honey
1 tablespoon orange juice

Slice bread, remove crusts and dry in slow oven for 20 minutes. Whip the cream lightly with the sugar, put in deep freeze for ½ hour. When bread has hardened grate into crumbs.
Melt the honey, add the orange juice and pour over the crumbs.
Mix the cream with the crumb mixture and mix well.
Freeze for 2 hours. This does not have to be turned out and whipped as it is low in water content.
For a dinner party use 2 tablespoons brandy instead of orange juice. One of our favourite ice-creams as it is so different. (Serves 6)

Christmas dinner, 1908

WINE JELLY

The party opposite have just finished their Christmas dinner. Wine, port and liqueurs have been served, the cigar-box lies open on the table.

The rattan sunblinds are down, so the day is probably a hot one, but the northern-hemisphere mid-day Christmas meal was dutifully consumed in New Zealand in Victorian and Edwardian times regardless of summer heat. In some households it persists to this day.

Hot roast turkey with all its traditional trimmings and a variety of vegetables, followed by plum pudding boiled in the wash-house copper. The kitchen staff tending the oven and the pots and pans covering the top of a glowing coal-fired range on a boiling hot day must have been close to heat-stroke.

The frozen-Christmas fantasy goes on and on. Shop windows are dotted with cottonwool snow, Santa Claus grievously perspires into his cottonwool beard, radio choirs intone "Jingle Bells" to listeners who can't imagine what a one-horse sleigh looks like, Christmas cards feature wistful robin redbreasts perched on frosty twigs of holly.

All very absurd. Also very endearing.

2 tablespoons powdered gelatine
6 tablespoons cold water
280 ml (½ pint) boiling water
190 ml (1/3 pint) port
190 ml (1/3 pint) white wine
190 ml (1/3 pint) orange and lemon juice
120 g (4 oz) sugar

Soak gelatine in cold water, dissolve in boiling water, add sugar and stir until dissolved.
Add fruit juice and wines.
Pour into a wetted mould.
Serve with whipped cream and fresh fruit.

PICKLE FOR BEEF OR PORK,

700 g (1½ lbs) sea salt or plain salt
240 g (8 oz) brown sugar
30 g (1 oz) saltpetre
4.5 l (1 gallon) water
1 doz juniper berries
4 bayleaves
1 tablespoon allspice
1 tablespoon black pepper

Put all ingredients into saucepan and simmer for 15 minutes.
Strain and use when cold.
The meat is put into the liquid and left from 5 to 7 days. It must
be turned every day and is best in a china or plastic container,
not metal. It should be well covered with a lid or muslin and kept
in a cool place—not the fridge.

*Salting, pickling or curing (i.e. to rub with salt granulated to the
size of wheat) meat to preserve it is a cookery practice as old as
ancient Egypt.*
*New Zealand's earliest immigrants were all too familiar with salt
meat because it was the main protein food on a long sea voyage.
Live sheep, pigs and poultry were carried on deck and slaughtered
one by one, but there was a limit to the number that a small
ship could carry and heavy seas could wash them overboard.*

*Salt meat then became the staple diet, along with dried pulses
and ship's biscuits.*
*When passenger traffic began in earnest the first-class travellers
had better fare and could supplement it with their own delicacies,
but for steerage folk salt beef was still the staple.*
*Once safely on land, a family still needed a brine tub; a sheep
could be eaten before pickling became necessary, but if a cattle-
beast or pig was slaughtered some of the meat had to be preserved.
On the remoter farms and in households which still take a pride
in following traditional methods, the brine tub is still in use.*
*Home-pickled beef and ham have a succulence too often absent
from the commercial product.*

Steam-engine in trouble, Nelson

EMS

The picture needs no words.

A set of heavy gem-irons is needed for these light gem scones, which are best served hot.

>   240 g (8 oz) self raising flour
>   60 g (2 oz) butter
>   60 g (2 oz) sugar
>   1 egg
>   1 teaspoon powdered ginger
>   250 ml (8 fluid oz) milk
>   pinch salt
>   butter for greasing

Pre-heat the gem irons in 400°F/200°C oven.
Cream the butter and sugar well, then beat in egg.
Fold in sifted sugar, flour and ginger, alternately with the milk.
Put ¼ teaspoon butter into each hot gem iron, then two-thirds fill with the mixture.
Cook in 400°F/200°C for 10–15 minutes until risen and golden brown.
Split and butter and eat warm.

GINGER BEER

1·3 kg (3 lbs) sugar
120 g (4 oz) ginger root
50 g (1½ oz) cream of tartar
1 teaspoon dried yeast
1 white of egg
9 l (2 gallons) boiling water
juice of 3 large lemons

Bruise the ginger well and boil it for 20 minutes in the water.
Add sugar, lemon juice and strain.
When cool, add cream of tartar, yeast and white of egg.
Stir well.
Let stand for 12 hours, then bottle and cork well.

An 1855 recipe for this specifies loaf *sugar, a term that persisted well into the present century though by then most people had forgotten its origin and could not have explained why so many conical hills in New Zealand are called "the Sugarloaf".*

In the 1840s and 1850s sugar was still being imported in solid loaf form. The loaf was conical or mitre-shaped and would weigh from two to twenty kilos. Country housewives would buy it ungrated, wholesalers and grocers would sell the produce ready grated.

A very coarse grating would produce brewer's crystals, *similar in texture to the coffee-crystal sugars of today. Ordinary household sugar would be sold as* loaf *or* grated. *A finer grating still would give the texture of fine sand suitable for use in a sugar-caster over fruit or pudding; this is still called* caster *(sometimes spelled* castor) *sugar. The finest grating was called, then as now,* icing *sugar.*

By the 1860s the sugarloaf had been replaced by the ready-grated sugars, but by then the many Sugarloaf Hills, always conical in shape, had been baptised.

Dew Drop Inn

CONFECTIONERY

The garden party is not what it was. Its main ingredient—a warm and sunny day—is still to be had, but the beautifully designed and meticulously tended private gardens of a hectare or more began to be subdivided after World War I. They demanded fulltime or jobbing gardeners, but the Age of Moneyed Leisure was on its way out.

Garden parties could be purely social affairs; sylvan stock-exchanges for the pursuit of gossip, scandal and discreet flirtation, with or without a game of croquet or lawn tennis thrown in as a bonus.

Or, as pictured here, the party might be dedicated to genteel fund-raising for the local church or some good charitable purpose. In this case the party would be less exclusive. The wives and families of tradesmen and workmen would be tolerated so long as they were prepared to buy—but they should not presume to cross the threshold of the hostess's house: that privilege was reserved for the socially acceptable.

The goods on sale were exactly what they are at the street-stall charitable fairs of today: homemade cakes and jams; discarded books and magazines; needlework for boudoir or linen cupboard. And sweets—which were still called lollies *by respectable people, while* candy *meant only candied fruits and their peels. Much loving care and ingenuity were lavished on the little frilly paper bags and boxes, and the sweet-stall made a charming picture—till the kids were let loose on it.*

46

BRANDY SNAPS

120 g (4 oz) white flour
120 g (4 oz) butter
120 g (4 oz) sugar
120 g (4 oz) treacle
1 teaspoon ground ginger
1 tablespoon of brandy

Melt the butter, sugar and treacle, brandy and ginger together in a saucepan.
When melted but not boiling pour over the sieved flour and stir well. The mixture should be runny.
Drop teaspoonfuls on greased tray 50 mm (2 in.) apart.
Bake at 350°F/180°C for 8–10 minutes.
Rub the handle of a wooden spoon with oil. When the snaps are cooked, remove with a palette knife and curl them round the handle of the spoon.
When cool fill with whipped cream.

HOKEY POKEY

4 tablespoons sugar
2 tablespoons golden syrup
1 teaspoon baking soda

Boil golden syrup and sugar for 7 minutes, then add baking soda.
(It will froth up to the top of the saucepan, so use a large one!)
Pour into buttered tin.
Break into pieces when cold.

Sweet-stall at a garden party, 1913

TEAKETTLE BROTH

1 loaf stale white bread, cut into 30 mm (1 in.) cubes
salt and pepper

Put cubed bread into warmed bowls, sprinkle with salt and
pepper to taste, and pour boiling water over till it almost covers
the cubes.

This recipe, though horrifying to a dietitian, tastes a lot more
interesting than it sounds and was thought nicer than nursery
bread-and-milk by some New Zealand children of 60 and more
years ago. It is also a traditional Welsh dish—if dish it can be
called.

*New Zealand first knew serious economic depression in 1865;
what historians have called the Long Depression began in that
year and continued with short intermissions until 1895. The next
depression began in 1922 and its severity tightened disastrously in
the worldwide economic crisis of 1930.*
*Businesses collapsed, unemployment was rife, the Government
organised relief work—very poorly paid. Much of it was stulti-
fying and pointless but at least it was work to be done and
better than what was happening in Britain, where for years men
rotted idle on the dole.*

*The men opposite have something more useful to do than the
chipping of weeds from streets, a particularly detested form of
relief work. The group may include unskilled workers, bankrupt
tradesmen, and ex-lawyers or accountants.*
*Recovery began in 1936 when the country's first Labour
Government was elected and initiated sweeping social reforms.
It is still argued that recovery was already on its way, and that
Labour's takeover was coincidental; but at the time the ex-
unemployed were convinced that Prime Minister Michael Savage
was the country's saviour.*

Depression, 1932

49

TEMPERANCE

"I must specially observe one point as to which the New Zealand colonist . . . far outpasses his Australian rival. He is very fond of getting drunk." So wrote visiting novelist Anthony Trollope in 1872.

In 1911, popular feeling favoured the total prohibition of liquor very nearly turned New Zealand dry; in the national referendum Prohibition gained a clear majority of 55.83 per cent, but a 60 per cent majority was needed to carry the day. In 1919 only a clear majority of over 50 per cent was needed but Prohibition polled only 49 per cent; soldiers still serving overseas voted overwhelmingly against it, and it was only their votes that kept New Zealand wet. In the 1966 referendum Prohibition polled but 16.7 per cent; observation of the great USA experiment had been disillusioning.

But though denied total victory the forces working for liquor reform and control are still much to be reckoned with. They have worked and are still actively working for any amendment that will help to reduce drunkenness. Many groups are concerned, the oldest and most influential being the Women's Christian Temperance Union, whose 1913 garden party in Nelson is seen opposite.

These ladies would have applauded the two teetotal recipes that follow. Harvesters and shearers develop powerful thirsts and although in earlier days some farmers provided beer or cider for their workers, the custom soon faded: men work better on a temperance brew. Besides, beer and cider were more expensive.

50

HARVEST BREW

> 30 g (1 oz) hops
> 30 g (1 oz) bruised ginger root
> sprig of mint
> 7 l (12 pints) water
> 450 g (1 lb) brown sugar

Boil the hops, ginger and mint in the water for 20 minutes.
Then add brown sugar and boil 10 minutes more.
Then strain and bottle when hot.
It will be ready for drinking when cold.

OATMEAL WATER

120 g (4 oz) fine oatmeal
180 g (6 oz) sugar
1 lemon cut into slices
4.5 l (8 pints) water, boiling

Mix all ingredients together well with a little warm water. Then add boiling water, stir, and use when cool.

Women's Christian Temperance Union meeting, 1913

CHINESE GOOSEBERRY FOOL

The intrepid motorist of the photograph could not have told you what a Chinese gooseberry was, for this fruit, like the tree-tomato or tamarillo, the feijoa and the avocado, was not grown in New Zealand—commercially, at any rate—until after World War II.

The Chinese gooseberry (Actinidia chinensis) *is a native of China's Yangtse Valley. The plant is a lusty and handsome creeper that will survive light frosts, and the flesh of the brown, hairy cylindrical fruit looks like and tastes rather like that of the common gooseberry.*

A few years ago a New Zealander exporting Chinese goose-berries was warned by his US agent that they were not selling well because Americans thought they must be produce of Red China. "Sell them as Kiwi fruit then," cabled the New Zealander, on the spur of the moment. But so far, this alternative name has not entirely taken on in this country.

2 eggs
¼ teaspoon salt
½ teaspoon vanilla
1 tablespoon cornflour
250 ml (1 cup) milk
90 g (3 oz) sugar
1 cup of cooked Chinese gooseberry
   pulp, well drained
½ cup whipped cream
raw Chinese gooseberries as a garnish

Separate the egg yolks and whites. Combine the yolks, salt, cornflour and vanilla, and add the milk gradually. Cook in double boiler until thick. Stir in half the sugar and leave to cool.

Beat the egg whites stiff, then beat in the rest of the sugar. Fold egg whites into cooled custard, then add fruit pulp and whipped cream.

Pile into serving dish and decorate with sliced Chinese goose-berries.

First car to drive from Wellington to Auckland, 1912

Eeling party, 1910

STEWED EELS

2 kg (4 lb) eel
570 ml (½ pint) dry red wine or stock
3 onions
2 bayleaves
30 g (1 oz) flour
30 g (1 oz) butter
juice of ½ lemon
3 whole allspice
pinch of salt, pepper, nutmeg
parsley

Skin the eels and cut into pieces 80 mm (3 in.) long. (If a black fat-gland is present, remove this.) Slice onions finely and fry in the butter until soft. Then gradually add the flour and stock (or red wine) stirring to make a smooth sauce. Then add seasonings, bayleaves, and pieces of eel. Simmer covered for about 45 minutes, taste sauce and add lemon juice and more salt if necessary. Serve with fried bread and sprinkled with chopped parsley.

Freshwater eels (Anguilla spp;) abound in our lakes, rivers and creeks. Specimens over 1.6 metres in length and of twenty kilos weight have been recorded, but as eel-catchers are eel-eaters and not much concerned with measurements, even longer and heavier eels may be common enough.

The Maori, like the London Cockney and the German gastronome, finds the eel prime eating, as have Pakeha bushmen and hunters accustomed to living off the land. But to citydwellers the eel looks sinister, and there may be an old unconscious prejudice against it as a food of the London slums.

Prejudice usually dies very hard; but there are signs that the eel may be wriggling its way into favour and on to the slabs of respectable fishmongers. An increasing number of people are finding smoked eel to be the delicacy that it undoubtedly is (and a profitable export to the Netherlands and Germany); and recipes such as the one given here will, if tried, win new converts.

WHITEBAIT FRITTERS

Most New Zealanders, if asked to name the choicest of the foods available only in this country, would vote for whitebait.

The adult whitebait (Galaxias attenuatus) *is a freshwater minnow averaging ten to fifteen centimetres in length. In autumn it moves downstream to the estuaries, where it lays its eggs among the aquatic vegetation. The eggs hatch and the larvae move out to sea, returning to the estuaries in the spring as transparent, thread-like creatures ten centimetres or so long.*

The whitebaiters' nets are waiting for them. The catch commands a price that has always been high; for the little fish that turn milk-white when cooked have a unique and delicate flavour.

The fritters and patties sold commercially are too often doughy wads with only a few token whitebait inside them. The following recipe does them full justice.

(serves 4)
180 g (6 oz) whitebait
2 eggs
1 teaspoon salt
pinch of pepper
2 tablespoons soft white breadcrumbs

Beat eggs well, then add other ingredients.
Heat some butter and fry tablespoon lots on both sides.
Serve with lemon slices.

Three in a tub

MUTTON PIE

480 g (1 lb) pastry, short or puff
480 g (1 lb) mutton, lean
1 onion
120 g (4 oz) mushrooms
2 sheep's kidneys
290 ml (½ pint) stock
a little flour, salt and pepper

Cut the meat into neat pieces, skin and core the kidneys and cut into strips. Roll meat and kidneys in seasoned flour (a brown plastic or paper bag with the seasoned flour in it is the easiest way). Line a piedish with the pastry and put the meat, finely chopped onion and sliced mushrooms in this. Season well, add a little of the stock. Cover with pastry, make a slit in the top and decorate with pastry leaves. Brush with milk and bake for 2 hours at 360°F/180°C. When crust is brown protect with greased paper. Ten minutes before serving fill up with rest of the stock.

Railway station, Te Aute

Lady in fancy dress

PAVLOVA CAKE

It is often claimed, and perhaps justly, that the "Pav" of affectionate parlance is New Zealand's first and only contribution to international cuisine—that is excluding foodstuffs native only to this country. The name of the benefactress who first created this festive and decorative example of meringue work may never be remembered; but the date was probably 1926, when the great ballerina toured this country, or shortly afterwards. Classical ballet had never been seen here until then, and Pavlova's presentation of The Dying Swan was talked about for years afterwards—as well it deserved to be.

The cake is too special for everyday serving. It looks extraordinarily elegant and festive when well decorated—as fragile and appealing as its namesake. And it tastes even better than it looks. Best held in reserve for ultra-special occasions.

It was christened in a happy hour, for a Pavlova is the prima ballerina assoluta of confectionery.

3 egg whites
180 g (6 oz) caster sugar
pinch of salt
1 teaspoon vinegar
1 teaspoon vanilla
1 teaspoon cornflour

Beat the egg whites stiffly with salt. Add caster sugar a teaspoonful at a time, beating continuously. Fold in vanilla, vinegar and cornflour.

Draw a circle 180 mm (7 in.) in diameter on a piece of greaseproof paper, and then hold it under the cold tap, shake off surplus water and smooth on to a cold oven tray. Pile the mixture into circle, keeping the sides a little higher than the centre.

Bake at 275°F/140°C until dry outside, turn over and remove paper. Return to oven until dry, about 1½ hours. Leave in oven until cool, decorate with whipped cream and fruit such as passionfruit pulp and strawberries, or Chinese gooseberries.

61

BAKED TROUT

Venator: On my word, master, this is a gallant trout: what shall we do with him?
Piscator: Marry, e'en eat him to supper.

So says Izaak Walton in his Compleat Angler, *and no good angler will neglect his advice.*
New Zealand offers both brown and rainbow trout, both most highly comestible. And the trout is as versatile in the kitchen as it is gallant in contending with its captor—a recent local cookery book gives forty-one recipes for trout and even these don't fully exhaust its potential.

"An angler's paradise" is a weary old hack of a phrase; but visiting anglers use it so often of our lakes and rivers that New Zealanders just smile and say "Yes".

1 medium-sized trout
salt
60 g (2 oz) butter
30 g (1 oz) flour
1 cup rich top milk (including liquor from baking the trout);
juice of one lemon

Clean and gut trout, sprinkle cavity with salt (and leave overnight if possible to develop flavour). Wrap in greaseproof paper (not waxed) then in several thicknesses of damp newspaper. Then in several thicknesses of dry newspaper. Put in a baking dish and bake at 350°F/180°C (1½–2 hours for a 2 kg fish).

Remove and unwrap fish.
Serve with lemon sauce as follows:

Melt butter in double boiler, stir in flour and seasoning, add milk and any liquor from trout and cook until mixture thickens, add lemon juice and blend well.

SHERBET

Family orchestras were commonplace in pre-Edison phonograph days, and many photographs similar to the one opposite survive in public photo-collections and private albums. (Another photo somewhat similar to the one opposite is that of the Pearse musical family of Temuka, South Canterbury, in 1897: in that case the piano has been carried bodily out into the garden, the eight instrumentalists include young Richard Pearse hugging his cello, and not one of them dreamed then that in six years' time Richard's crazy aeroplane would lumber off the ground nine months before Wilbur and Orville Wright would achieve powered flight.)

What sort of music did the family attempt? It can seldom have been anything very ambitious—the youth of the performers would see to that; Thomas Moore's 'Tis the Last Rose of Summer, Stephen Foster's Camptown Races, simple arias from the Gilbert and Sullivan operas? Richard Pearse's cello in later life consoled his darkening days with Gounod's Ave Maria.

The phonograph began to take over, radio was deadlier still to do-it-yourself music. For a while it looked as though television had killed it off for good and all.

The skiffle groups of twenty years ago proved that personal music might survive; and there are probably more guitar-playing teenagers today than there were piano-playing teenagers in 1900.

120 g (4 oz) tartaric acid
120 g (4 oz) carbonate of soda
360 g (12 oz) caster sugar
1 teaspoon powdered ginger
16 drops of essence of lemon scattered over the above.

Mix all ingredients well and bottle. Cork securely to keep the mixture dry. Use one teaspoonful to a tumblerful of cold water.

The McAllister family

Canteen kitchen, Piha

MIXED MEAL BREAD

Home breadmaking, like home musicmaking, saw a surprising revival in the early 1970s.
Man and Woman in incipient revolt against the Machines? If so, Samuel Butler was prophetic when he located Erewhon *in this country.*
The bread in this recipe is one that the authors make every week.

Wet Mix: (collect in large bowl)
450 g (1 lb) plain white flour
15 g (½ oz) dried yeast
1 teaspoon sugar
850 ml (1½ pints) warm water

Make into batter, beating well.
Leave in warm place until bubbly—15—20 minutes.

Dry Mix: (collect into basin)
450 g (1 lb) wholemeal flour coarse
240 g (½ lb) rye flour
240 g (½ lb) stoneground wholemeal flour (fine)
1 level tablespoon salt
1 level tablespoon sugar
2 tablespoons oil

Add dry mix to bubbly batter. Mix, knead in bowl until the dough can come cleanly out without any being left in the bowl.
Knead on greased board for 5 minutes until silky.
Then put dough into greased bowl and cover with large plastic bag closed with rubber band.
Leave at room temperature until doubled in bulk.
Knock back by flattening dough by hand and shape into loaves to fit three bread tins. (Dough should fill 2/3rds of the tin.)
Put tins in the large plastic bag and leave to rise in a warm place until the dough reaches the top of the tin. Remove plastic bag.
Pre-heat oven to 450°F/230°C and bake for 45 minutes.
The loaves should then be loose in the tins.
Put on rack to cool.

(Makes three loaves about 680 g (1½ lbs) each.)

Swagger, circa *1900*

THE LONERS

We have always had a floating population of homeless men. Possum-trappers, deer-cullers, forest firewatchers work singly or in couples. Gold-prospectors too, though there aren't many of them now; the West Coasters called the determinedly solitary prospector a hatter, *thinking perhaps of Alice's Hatter and March Hare.*

In the hard times men roamed the roads genuinely looking for regular paid work on the farms. And there have always been the swaggers proper, men who might work just long enough to earn the price of a few drinks but who generally bludged their way from farm to farm, begging or stealing eggs, fruit and vegetables.

Men living in rough huts or in barns and haystacks lived largely off the land and evolved their own crude cuisine. The swagger in the photograph has a blackened billy as his sole cooking-vessel: clasp-knife, fork and spoon, one each, are all he will use as utensils. In his blanket-roll or his pockets may be salt, tea, sugar, and tobacco, a cake of soap, a box of matches, scissors and, if he is a dandy, a comb.

The farmer and his wife will give him a meal in return for an odd job or two. This is mainly from natural pity, but also from what may happen if a meal is not offered: a swagger who has been refused food may say, "Matches are cheap, boss," and glance meaningfully towards the farmer's woolshed. Woolsheds burn easy.

EELS

A bushman's method of cooking eel is quick and easy. Directly it has been caught place it whole, uncleaned and unskinned, on the hot embers of a camp fire or a piece of hot iron. After some minutes it will turn itself inside out and the flesh can be removed in sections leaving bones and skin behind.

OPOSSUMS

These are skinned and cleaned like rabbits, but the backbone from the tail end upward for about 130 mm (5 in.) should be removed. (This contains a gland which taints the flesh if left in.) It can then be jointed and stewed like a rabbit, or roasted with fat bacon slices on it, and can be as tender as chicken—so some of the old bushmen say.

DAMPER (in camp oven)

900 g (2 lbs) flour
1 teaspoon bicarbonate of soda
2 teaspoons of cream of tartar
cold water

Mix all ingredients together, then slowly add enough cold water to make a firm but soft dough.
Knead for a few minutes to get some air into it.
Then shape into a circular loaf 60 mm (2 in.) thick.
Grease the camp oven and place loaf in it, leave for 15 minutes in a warm place, if possible.
Then place camp oven into the camp fire and cover the lid with hot ashes.
Leave for 35 minutes. Then test by thumping the bread. If it sounds hollow it is ready.

SCOTS OR SCOTCH EGGS

8 hardboiled eggs
2 raw eggs
700 g (1½ lb) pork sausagemeat
120 g (4 oz) crisp breadcrumbs
pinch of mace, salt and pepper
1 teaspoon grated lemon rind
oil for deep frying

Boil 8 eggs hard, run under tap to cool and then shell them.
Beat up 1 egg and add 1 tablespoon cold water.
Add the seasonings, lemon rind and mace to the sausagemeat.
Dip the hardboiled eggs into the beaten egg and cover each one entirely with the sausagemeat, pressing it on with the hands. Then beat up remaining egg and gently roll them in this, then dip in to the breadcrumbs, pressing them into the sausagemeat. Have the oil hot and fry them singly until they are golden brown. Drain well, and serve hot with mustard or cold with salad.

The drover's profession dated back to the earliest days of mankind, but within a few brief years it was brushed off the roads by the great double-decker stock trucks that thunder down the motorways.

When stock had to be moved long distances across country the farmer or one of his staff might undertake the job, but it was a specialised business and more often a fulltime drover was called in. He had to know the country, he had to be a good and patient stockman, physically tough for the long, slow treks, and—above all—a good man with dogs. His living depended on them. (More often than not he was also a redoubtable beer-drinker: stock on the move create a fog of dust, and hence a parching thirst.)

The sheepdog is not without honour in New Zealand, for the country could not, and cannot, do without him. He is seen at his astonishing best when competing at a dog trial, and visitors are well advised not to leave us without going to watch one. The rapport between dog and master must be seen to be believed.

The summer-siesta men in the photograph are farmers or drovers. It would be safe to bet that the main topic of their conversation is—dogs.

Frasertown, 1899

HANGI

(As described by the Rev. William Yate in An Account of New Zealand, 1835.)

"A circular hole is dug in the ground, rounded at the bottom like the inside of a basin; this is filled with dry firewood and small stones.

When the stones are heated to redness, they are taken out of the oven, and the place cleared from any remains of burning wood; a part of the hot stones are then placed in the oven again; and a wreath of damp leaves is laid round the outside, to prevent the earth from falling in, or the food from rolling to the side.

The potatoes are put in wet and any other vegetable placed upon the top of them; if animal food is to be cooked hot stones are put inside, to ensure it being properly done.

The whole being in the oven, a quantity of fresh leaves are laid over, over which are placed a few natives' baskets made of flax; a calabash full of water is then poured over the top, which causes the steam to arise; and all is immediately covered with earth, till none of the steam is seen to escape.

They judge very exactly the time when the animal food is done, and the sign of the vegetable matter being sufficiently cooked is the steam beginning to penetrate through the earth with which the oven is covered.

Dig a hole about 0.5 m (18 in.) deep, keeping the pile of dirt neatly to one side. Now comes the lining of the hole with stones. These stones have to withstand heat without cracking or exploding. Smooth stones from the seashore or river are not suitable, the best hangi stones are found in fast-flowing rivers, the rough jagged ones usually deep in the mud. Ask the local hangi expert in your district what he uses.

Line the hole with the stones.

Light a wood fire, a fierce dry heat is needed so use dry wood. Wait until the stones are hot enough for the water to run off in globules when you flick it on. Then remove the fire, brush the stones clear of ashes, and remove any charred pieces of wood-brush left unburned, as this would give a smoky taste to the food.

As everything is going to be cooked for the same length of time, make sure the meat is in small portions or, if it is a roast, half-cook it in an oven beforehand.

Wrap food in green leaves. Cabbage or silverbeet are suitable, or vineleaves if you can get them. If cooking fish, green seaweed is good. Vegetables are peeled and prepared in the normal way.

A little water can be poured on to start the steaming, then cover the food with clean wet tea-towels and then wet sacks. Then cover completely with the pile of dirt. Cover any steam vents when they occur.

Vegetables and fish will be done in 40–60 minutes, half-cooked joints or meat in small pieces will be done in 2 hours, big un-cooked joints will take about 4 hours.

Make sure while you are waiting that your company is convivial.

Maori ladies at Nelson, 1912

FREEMAN & SONS
BAKERS.
FREEMAN'S
Freeman's
WAIMEA ST.
BAKERS.
BAKERS
Freeman's
Freeman's
BAKERS
BAKERS

SOURDOUGH RYE BREAD

The baker's man called daily at city houses, bringing to the back door an assortment of warm loaves in his basket. Before the advent of motor-van and motorcycle he drove a light two-wheeled horse-van—often a spankingly smart turnout, for the tradesmen's van classes at agricultural and pastoral shows were keenly contested. The public watched the parade with great interest, and it was a matter for rejoicing if "your" baker or butcher was victorious.

Sourdough Paste:
3 tablespoons rye flour
3 tablespoons warm milk

Mix to a smooth paste the flour and warm milk and leave covered in a warm place for 2 days until it smells sour.

Bread:
720 g (1½ lbs) rye flour
480 g (1 lb) plain white flour
4 teaspoons salt
120 g (4 oz) melted butter
570 ml (1 pint) warm milk
15 g (½ oz) dried yeast
the sourdough paste as above
cream for glaze

Put both flours and salt into bowl.
Heat milk to blood heat, put in melted butter, sourdough paste and dried yeast, mix well with flour in bowl.
Knead into smooth silky dough, usually takes about 5–10 minutes, should leave hands clean.
Put into greased bowl, cover with large plastic bag and leave to rise until doubled in size.
Knead the dough once again and shape into two sausage shapes to fill two bread tins.
Put into greased tins, cover with plastic bag once again and leave until risen to the top of the tins.
Bake in hot oven 425°F/220°C for 30 minutes, then brush with cream and return to 350°F/180°C oven for another 40 minutes; should be loose in tins when done.

Baker's delivery circa 1926

HARE

New Zealand has no foxes, so only the hare is hunted with hounds. The importation of foxes to reduce the rabbit pest was once seriously debated but the colonists had by that time come to realise that the indiscriminate acclimatisation of exotic animals and plants could have unforeseen and disastrous consequences.

The hare is no friend of the farmer's. Bigger than a rabbit, he eats more pasture; but at no time has he multiplied as have rabbits, red deer and opossums.

Hare is sold by some fishmongers, but has never been highly valued for the New Zealand table. This is surprising, for although somewhat strongly flavoured it makes an excellent soup, braise or stew, and is particularly appetising if baked as in the following recipe.

A hare should be hung for 24—48 hours before skinning and removal of the entrails. When cleaning the animal be sure to remove the thin muscular membrane extending from the flank over the intestines. It is this membrane which if left in gives the hare an objectionably strong flavour.

Stuff the hare with your favourite stuffing.
In the old days it was covered with a thick paste of flour and water, but today it can be covered with aluminium cooking foil or put in a cooking bag.
Cook slowly in a baking dish for 2—3 hours depending on the size of the hare, in a moderate oven 300°F/150°C. If not covered while cooking it is inclined to be dry.

Styx Gun Club, Waimairi County

MUTTON HAM

Mutton ham is a most palatable alternative to pork ham. The lean meat does not have the rosy-pink colour of pork ham, being darkish-brown, but the flavour is very similar and is in fact preferred by many. Mutton has the additional advantage of being a great deal less expensive than pork.

Not many butchers offer mutton ham all the year round, but it is traditional Christmas fare and easily procurable in December.

Alternatively if you pickle it at home, using the following recipe, you can adjust the flavouring of spices and herbs exactly to your liking.

1 shoulder or leg of lamb, hogget, or mutton
120 g (4 oz) brown sugar
120 g (4 oz) sea salt if possible, or plain salt
1 dessertspoon powdered cloves
1 teaspoon pepper
1 teaspoon ground ginger
1 teaspoon ground mace

Mix all ingredients except the salt, and rub well into the meat. Let stand for about 2 hours and then rub in the salt. Place in large china container with lid, and turn meat twice a day for 6 days. Cook as for ham, soaking joint in cold water for a couple of hours before cooking. Then place in lukewarm water to which you have added some peppercorns and a bunch of fresh herbs. Simmer slowly, allowing 25 minutes per half kilo and an additional 25 minutes.

Tongariro National Park

KUMARA

Kumara is the Maori name used by all New Zealanders for the sweet potato (Ipomoea batatas), brought to this country in the ocean-going canoes of the early Polynesian settlers. The plant is of the convolvulus family and it is the fleshy tuber, in appearance not unlike the European potato, that is eaten.

For a hundred years and more ethnologists and archaeologists have been arguing about how Polynesia was first populated—whether from South America or from Malaysia—and the humble kumara has been put in the witness-box by people such as Thor (Kon-Tiki) Heyerdahl who favour the South American origin, as

Ipomoea is a plant native to Central and South America.

It is a subtropical plant, grown commercially in the northern districts of the North Island and sold by greengrocers in all parts of the country. The cooked flesh is orange in colour, soft, and decidedly sweet. It may be served as a root vegetable to accompany meat, with or as a substitute for ordinary potatoes. Either way, it is excellent eating and deservedly popular with Maori and Pakeha alike.

The word kumara is pronounced with the stress on the first syllable, as in camera.

Kumara and Apple:
450 g (1 lb) kumara, boiled and cut into 5 mm (¼ in.) pieces
120 g (4 oz) brown sugar
4 cooking apples, sliced thin
4 tablespoons butter
1 teaspoon salt

Butter a baking dish, put in alternative layers of kumara, then apple, sprinkling each layer with salt and sugar and dotting with butter. Repeat until all the ingredients are used up. Bake one hour in 350°F/180°C oven. (Serves 6)

Candied Kumaras:
4 medium-size kumaras
240 g (½ lb) dark brown sugar
140 ml (¼ pint) water
30 g (1 oz) butter
strained juice of one lemon
pinch of nutmeg and allspice

Cook kumaras in boiling water for 25-30 minutes, then drain, peel and slice them.
Mix sugar with water and all the other ingredients including spices, and bring to the boil.
Stir until the syrup thickens, then add kumara slices and boil for 5 minutes. (Serves 4)

Maori's washday

81

HOMEMADE BITTER BEER

Homebrewing came in with the first settlers and has been a popular pastime ever since. The product is a great deal cheaper than commercial beer but its strength and flavour are wildly variable. Good homebrew can be a splendid beverage: bad homebrew is terrible.

Guests invited by their host to sample his homebrew will do well to proceed with caution till they have got the hang of it.

1.3 kg (3 lbs) malt extract
450 g (1 lb) sugar
90 g (3 oz) hops
1 teaspoon dried yeast
½ teaspoon epsom salts
18 l (4 gallons) water

Equipment:

One 22 l (5 gal) plastic dustbin
One muslin bag
One 1.5 mm (5 ft) length of 10 mm (½ in.) plastic tube
24 clean beerbottles and crown tops
0.5 m (18 in.) thin dowel
2 rubber bands

Place the hops in a muslin bag or nylon stocking.
Bring 4 l (1 gal) of the water to boil and stir in the sugar, epsom salts and malt. Add the bag of hops and let the whole simmer for 30 minutes.

Meanwhile put 13 l (3 gal) of hot water in the plastic dustbin. Remove the bag of hops and pour the boiled mixture into the dustbin. Cover and leave overnight.

First thing in the morning, scatter 1 teaspoon of dried yeast over the surface of the beer, re-cover and leave. The rest depends on the weather. In about 4 days in winter, and less in the summer, a thick foam forms on the surface. Skim off with a wooden spoon and re-cover with lid. The liquid is muddy-looking at this time.

Check daily and when further foam forms, skim it off and re-cover. After about 4 to 7 days the liquid is clear. With the plastic tube siphon the beer into the bottles, avoiding the sediment settled at the bottom. Before attaching the crown top put ¼ teaspoon of sugar into each bottle.

This beer is drinkable in a week.
Be careful when decanting into glasses that the sediment at the bottom of the bottle does not get poured out also.
If added before the dried yeast, the juice of half a lemon and a cup of cold tea are a refinement.
All utensils and bottles should be perfectly clean.
Attach the plastic tube to the piece of thin dowelling by rubber bands, and this will avoid siphoning any sediment into the bottles.

83

HAND LOTION

Anyone who spends much time looking at social photographs of pre-1920 vintage may form the conclusion that New Zealanders liked to indulge, in the open, in pastimes that are more usually carried on indoors. We have already seen one example of this in the family-orchestra photo—where a sizeable harmonium has been hauled out of the livingroom and set up under the trees.

New Zealanders have always indeed been an outdoor people and may have preferred in the old days to make music or play cards out in the garden; if so, the practice has all but vanished. The more likely explanation is that good indoor photography was for the expert only. Early flashlight equipment was primitive and dangerous, and if mishandled could lead to spectacularly disconcerting results; and the glass-plate amateur photographer had no exposure-meter to advise him. Hence if the family was to be recorded in some indoor social occupation the photograph had to be taken out of doors.

In the matter of indoor games New Zealand follows international fashion. The old long-term stalwarts, whist and euchre, yielded to auction bridge, though these old games are still played competitively in some towns and country districts. Mah-jong sets spawned like mushrooms in the early 1920s but have long since been forgotten. Radio and television made great inroads into family games, but the 1960s saw a startling resurgence of the ancient and noble game of chess; and in 1976 the Government is meditating legislation to control commercial housie (lotto), a nursery toy to the Victorians but now a feverish if relatively innocuous form of adult gambling.

What game is being played by the family opposite? If it is poker, the gentleman in the high-backed chair seems likely to make a killing.

juice 3 lemons
same quantity of glycerine
same quantity of boracic lotion
(made by dissolving 1 teaspoon of boracic acid powder in a cup
of boiling water)
1 tablespoon olive oil
1 tablespoon white methylated spirits

84   Mix all together and bottle tightly.

Family cards

PUHA (RAURIKI OR SOW-THISTLE)

Puha *and* rauriki *are the Maori names for a native sow-thistle* (Sonchus oleraceus), *used as a green vegetable long before European settlement and still popular with Polynesian people. Few Pakehas now trouble to explore its culinary qualities, but in the early days it was not despised: it had, and has, the great advantage of growing wild and plentifully, so there was no bother·of cultivating it. In flavour and cooked texture it has affinities with spinach.*

Until the potato was introduced the Maori's staple source of carbohydrate food was aruhe, *or native bracken-fern root, which required long and laborious preparation to make it edible. Like puha it grew wild and profusely and did not demand the cultivation required by kumara and taro. Other starchy foods included the pith of the mamaku tree fern* (Cyathea medullaris), *and of the ti-tree or cabbage tree* (Cordyline australis).

Green vegetables included puha and the young leaves of the five-finger tree (Neopanax arboreum).

Curiously, the Maori seem to have made no use of two native green vegetables that the European found a use for. One is what Captain James Cook found to be a useful specific for the vitamin C deficiency-disease scurvy, all too familiar to mariners on long ocean voyages; what he named "scurvy-grass" is the native Lepidium oleraceum, *now virtually extinct. The other is the extremely nutritious New Zealand spinach* (Tetragonia tetragonioides), *a hardy and easily cultivated ground-cover plant of somewhat rougher texture than the common spinach of the northern hemisphere but very palatable. The seeds are available commercially here and in Britain at the more enterprising seedsmen's shops.*

The little girl of this gently-smiling mother seems to be eating candy floss, a spun-sugar confection endemic at agricultural and pastoral shows and similar festivities.

Wash puha thoroughly. Put into boiling water and boil for 5 minutes. Rinse under cold running water, then return to boiling water and cook for about ½ hour or until the bitterness is gone. Drain thoroughly.

Lightly steamed mussels may be cut into pieces, mixed with puha and served with mashed potato. Pork bones or pork strips are often cooked with puha and it usually takes about ¾ hour for the meat to cook thoroughly. The liquid left makes a base for soup if left overnight, the fat then removed, and a few vegetables added.

Thermal area, 1893

HOT PUNCH

To spend a summer holiday "taking the waters" at a thermal spa was highly fashionable in eighteenth and nineteenth century Europe. One submitted to the regime prescribed by the local specialist, drinking and bathing in the water and following a spartan dietary that gave a usually overworked liver something of a holiday too.
New Zealand is wealthy in thermal springs, those of Rotorua being the best known, and nineteenth-century doctors believed implicitly in their therapeutic value.

(Serves 8—10)

2.3 l (4 pints) red wine
280 ml (½ pint) brandy
1 orange, diced
1 lemon, diced
1 orange stuck with 20 cloves
4 cinnamon sticks
½ teaspoon grated nutmeg

Slowly heat all these ingredients until very hot but not boiling. Serve in small thick glasses.

FARMHOUSE BREAD

The air-passenger looking down at forest or bare mountain might well imagine the country beneath him to be uninhabited by man. He cannot see the many tracks and huts built for and by trampers and hunters, foresters and trappers, climbers and musterers.

The hut interior here is very typical. The fireplace and chimney are in corrugated iron, camp oven and billy are on the hearth. The walls are decorated with pictures from the old Auckland Weekly, Freelance or Weekly Press, and probably there are doggerel verses scribbled up here and there. Here men may shelter for a night or stay for several days, weatherbound.

Catering has been made a lot simpler by the advent of pre-cooked, canned and dehydrated foods, but many New Zealand men enjoy cooking and can turn on an excellent meal from a few basic ingredients.

In the Middle East campaigns of World War II, British army catering officers recorded astonishment at the ingenuity of New Zealand troops in devising desert-cooking equipment and the ability of most of them to knock up a really good meal from army rations.

1.3 kg (3 lbs) flour
1 dessertspoon salt
1 dessertspoon lard or butter
1 tablespoon sugar
280 ml (½ pint) homemade yeast. See page 100.
or 15 g (½ oz) dried yeast
570 ml (1 pint) milk and water

Heat milk and water. Add sugar and lard, cool to lukewarm add yeast and 450 g (1 lb) flour, beat until smooth. Cover, and leave in warm place until foamy.
Add salt to the remaining flour and add to yeast mixture to form a firm dough, which comes from the bowl cleanly. Knead on lightly greased board until elastic and smooth.
Return dough to greased bowl, moisten the top with water. Cover and leave to rise until doubled in bulk.
Knead lightly once again and form into loaves. Place in greased loaf tins or a well greased camp oven, cover and allow to rise to twice its bulk again.
Bake in hot oven 450°F/230°C for 45—50 minutes for 450 g (1 lb) loaves, (longer for larger loaves) or until they are loose in the tins. Brush with milk just before removing from oven.

VELVET CREAM

The New Zealand woman is as sports-minded as her brother and, with the present exception of rugby football and boxing, there is no sport that is not played by both sexes. You name it, women play it.

A competitive pastime so far reserved for ladies only is the curious phenomenon of marching girls. *Teams of a dozen or so, dressed in stylish and colourful drum-majorette uniforms, march to music and perform complex patterns of manoeuvre with a snappy precision that has been known to make a retired Guards drill-sergeant almost speechless with admiration.*

The first recorded mention of women's hockey is at Nelson in 1897, only a year or two after it was first played by men in this country.

30 g (1 oz) gelatine
280 ml (½ pint) of sherry
570 ml (1 pint) of cream
rind and juice of two lemons
180 g (6 oz) sugar

Soak the gelatine in the sherry, then dissolve by gently heating and stirring all the time. Grate the lemon peel into the sherry and then add the juice together with the sugar. Then pour the mixture very gently into the cream, stirring until cold. Then put into wetted mould.

from cookery book sold in aid of the Hastings District Plunket Nurse Society, 1912

Hockey tournament 1910

HOMEMADE PORK SAUSAGES

The wild pig is a villain. Captain Cook liberated his ancestors, domestic pigs that would give the Maori a badly-needed supplement to his protein foods, and inevitably a few escaped and became bushrangers.

In districts where wild pigs are numerous they are detested by farmers, as they kill and devour young lambs and will turn a snug vegetable patch into chaos overnight. And, though not as destructive to forests as are opossums, deer and wild goats, they play their part in that wicked work.

Pighunting is done with "two dogs and a rifle", and is claimed by its devotees to be a more sporting exercise than deerstalking: an old boar bailed up against a tree will fight savagely for his life, and the hunter and his dogs are at real risk.

Wild pork carries less fat than the domestic kind and has a more positive flavour. It is used exactly as domestic pork—which is not surprising, as the wild pig of New Zealand is not feral, as is the wild pig of Asia for example, but is a descendant of the domestic breed.

1 tart apple peeled and grated
about ½ loaf stale bread minced or grated
340 g (1½ lb) pork pieces
½ teaspoon ground nutmeg
1 beaten egg
1 tablespoon chopped parsley
pepper and salt

Mince pork finely and then bread, mix all other ingredients, season well, bind with beaten egg.
Form into sausages and fry until brown.

Bowls, Stratford

MARROWBONES

Who breathes that bowls not? What bold tongue can say
Without a blush, he has not bowl'd today?
It is the trade of men, and every sinner
Has play'd his rubber; every bowl's a winner.
The vulgar proverb's crost, he hardly can
Be a good bowler and an honest man.

This was the opinion of Francis Quarles, a minor poet in King Charles the First's time. Untrue of New Zealand bowlers an honest and a dedicated group, most of them on the autumnal side of fifty. Bowls probably has more players than any other sport; in 1962 there were two bowlers for every one golfer.

The prescribed uniform—panama hat with the club's name on the ribbon, dark blue blazer and immaculate white trousers or skirt—is so universally worn that some social critics have discerned in it evidence of a national inclination towards conformity and regimentation.

It has not always been so. By modern standards the bowlers in this photograph are disgracefully dressed and would be warned off the green for life.

Marrowbones—who serves them nowadays? In the days when the sweet course was followed by a savoury which, in turn, preceded dessert (raw fruit and nuts), marrowbones were a popular savoury, served swaddled in a snow-white napkin, cradled in a silver dish, accompanied by a long thin silver scoop with which to dig the marrow from the bone.

The scoops still turn up occasionally at auctions and in antique shops, but few people now know what they were used for. Like buttonhooks and curling-tongs, they are rather triste *reminders of more spacious days. Marrowbones are now so seldom asked for that some butchers will not only cut them in half for you, they will let you have them for nothing. Surprising: marrow is delicious.*

Large shank beef bones, which you might be able to persuade your butcher to cut into short lengths, if he is not too busy.

flour
dry toast
slices of lemon

Seal the ends of the bones with thick paste of flour and water. Tie them into floured cloth and boil for 1½ to 2 hours. Remove cloth and paste from ends. Serve upright on hot dish with dry toast and slices of lemon.

MAORI CORN

George French Angas visited New Zealand in 1846 and was not enamoured of the Maori way with corn: "The cobs of maize are placed in flax baskets and put under water for some weeks, until quite putrid; then taken out and made into . . . disgusting cakes. At other times the putrid mass is converted into a sort of gruel that sends forth an effluvia (sic) over the whole settlement."

The following recipe warns you of the smell; but had the Maori hosts of Mr Angas presented him with the "putrid" gruel served as advised, he would not have been so scathing about it. As with durian fruit and Stilton cheese, an evil smell may mask a most palatable taste.

For this recipe you need access to a clear running stream.
1 clean sugarbag
water
½ teaspoon salt
1.3 kg (3 lb) sweet-corn kernels

Remove the husks and let dry in the sun until cobs are hard. Then put into sugarbag, and put into clear running water, making sure to fasten bag to the bank securely. Leave for 2–3 months, then strip the corn from the cob. This will now smell very strongly. Wash thoroughly and boil for about 1 hour in lots of water, then simmer for another 1½ hours. You will have to add water from time to time to make sure it does not boil dry or stick to the bottom.
Add ½ teaspoon salt when thick, then serve hot with cream and brown sugar.

Family group

HOMEMADE YEAST

Homebrewing is a popular pastime with many New Zealand men, who at one time bitterly resented the arrangement whereby the commercial breweries bought the entire crop of hops and would not allow the grower to sell his good-quality hops to outsiders. Happily, the homebrewer can now buy good average quality hops for his potions.

Hops were at first grown all over the country but their commercial growing, like that of tobacco, is now concentrated in the Waimea County of Nelson. The growing crops and the farmers' kilns give the landscape a distinctive attraction.

The use of hops is not wholly confined to beer. The true-blue back-to-Nature home-baker scorns the use of commercial yeasts and prefers to make his or her own, following one of the old colonial recipes. One of the constant worries of the pioneer housewife was a steady supply of yeast when unable to obtain baker's yeast or French or German yeast (a form of dried yeast). The following recipe was commonly used.

15 g (½ oz) dried hops
1 l (1 quart) cold water
3 tablespoons flour
3 tablespoons brown sugar
few raisins

Boil hops in cold water for 20 minutes. Strain and cool. Blend the flour and sugar to a smooth paste with a little of this liquid then add the remainder. Bottle, and to each bottle add 2 raisins. Cork securely, tying corks down. Stand in warm place for 24 hours when it should be ready for use. Store in cool place thereafter.

Hop-pickers

Singsong, Chatham Islands

MUTTONBIRDS

Muttonbird is the chick of the sooty shearwater (Puffinus griseus), *which nests in burrows on the offshore islands of New Zealand and on similar islands in Australia's Bass Strait.*

The ancient Maori ate them, as do his descendants and some Pakehas. They are on sale in most fish-shops but are seldom if ever served in hotels and restaurants—the reason for this being that they smell very strongly, though not unpleasantly, during cooking. For the same reason many housewives avoid buying them.

If they are cooked out of doors this objection vanishes. The flesh is very tasty: "a cross between chicken and kipper" is how a visitor from Britain might describe it.

TO COOK MUTTONBIRDS (SMOKED)

Wash in warm water, and put on to cook in hot water. Cover pan with lid.
Simmer slowly for 30 minutes with window open, or out of doors.
Remove from water and wipe dry.
Open the bird and with the fat uppermost grill on wire rack until most of the fat has been extracted.
Serve with sliced lemon and potato baked in its jacket.

MUTTONBIRD PASTE

Simmer bird until flesh can be removed from the bones, discarding any skin and fat.
Pass twice through the mincer and add a little anchovy essence or sauce and season to taste.
Put into small jars and store in fridge.

MUTTONBIRD (FRESH)

To grill:

Wipe the bird with a damp cloth, spread open with the fat uppermost on a wire rack.
Grill slowly until the fat is extracted.
Turn for the last few minutes of cooking.

To roast:

Put on a wire rack in a baking tin with fat side uppermost.
Bake in a medium oven for about half an hour, until fat has been extracted. (If the bird is allowed to cook in the fat the flesh is oily and the flavour too strong.)
If eaten hot serve with apple sauce. If cold, with tomato and cucumber salad.

103

GRILLED VENISON STEAKS

The red deer is the country's most controversial animal. Importation began in 1851 and continued until 1924, but by the latter date the numbers had got out of hand and it was recognised that the deer were doing serious damage to native forests, with soil erosion and flooding as a consequence.

Conservationists favoured total extermination, and the Government paid men to cull the herds to extinction-point – but the nature of mountain and forest terrain made this impracticable. The deerstalkers, naturally, were up in arms against the extermination policy, pointing out that the sport attracted a considerable number of overseas visitors. They conceded that selective culling to encourage the breeding of world-quality trophies would be acceptable.

The advent of the helicopter and the high overseas price for venison introduced a new and even more controversial element.

Paid cullers were not needed when airborne meat-hunters wrangled with each other over the most profitable areas; strife developed between the meat-hunters, the trophy stalkers, the conservationists, and those who were shocked by a television programme portraying the ruthless methods of the helicopter operators. A policy acceptable to all parties is inconceivable, and at the time of writing the debate is continuing. Hotly.

Venison is served in some hotels and restaurants but is not often on sale in the shops. It is not wonderfully popular in private homes, many people considering it an unacceptably dry meat; so a food treated as a high luxury in older and more populous countries goes mostly for export.

Cooked as here advised, venison steaks are indeed worthy of the homage paid them by the gastronomes of Europe.

2 venison steaks from back or leg from a young animal
salt and pepper
olive oil
red currant jelly

Beat steaks lightly to flatten, season with salt and pepper. Put into dish, cover with olive oil and let stand for 3 hours. Then drain and grill 10 minutes on each side until well done. Serve with red currant jelly.

Tongariro National Park

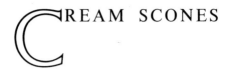REAM SCONES

It is often said that New Zealand cooks excel in the making of breads, cakes and scones but that their cuisine is less strong in the meat, fish and vegetable departments.

Various reasons have been put forward for this. One is the Scottish influence on New Zealand cookery, and it is a fact that the Scot outshines the Englishman in flour-cookery. Also, that the country cook usually had unlimited good mutton at her disposal, and fresh vegetables, so the cookery of these commodities was not a challenge to her skill and imagination; whereas breads, cakes and scones had to be made and were not to be bought— hence specialisation on them became a social tradition.

Scones lend themselves to short-notice entertaining, and there are literally dozens of local recipes for them that include the use of apples, pumpkin, cheese, dates—practically anything off the kitchen shelf can be thrust upon the agreeably versatile basic scone mixture. The recipe given is unusual but a good one.

450 g (1 lb) flour
4 tablespoons butter, softened
4 teaspoons baking powder
280 ml (½ pint) creamy milk (can be half cream and half water)
2 eggs beaten
pinch of salt

Sift all dry ingredients together, then rub butter in lightly.
Mix with knife eggs and cream liquid and dry ingredients to a fairly soft dough.
Tip on to floured board, roll lightly to 2 mm (¾ in.) thick and cut into rounds.
Bake in hot oven 450°F/230°C for 8–12 minutes.

This is a richer mixture than most and keeps for a few days. Nice with homemade raspberry jam and clotted or whipped cream.

Afternoon tea, Dunedin

TAMARILLO PORK

New Zealand's old mailcoaches were, and are, often referred to as Cobb & Co. coaches, but in fact the firm of Cobb & Co. never operated outside Australia. It was started by the American Freeman Cobb and two compatriots in Victoria. The error is pardonable, for when at the time of the Central Otago goldrush an Australian coachman named Cole brought a coach to this country he went into business as "Cobb & Co. C.C. Cole & Co., proprietors". Other coaching firms followed suit though they too had no connection of any kind with the Australian firm.

About 1903 an appreciative traveller recorded the start of a South Island coach trip: "The horses arrive in beautiful formation. Three leaders, two polers, like well-drilled soldiers, eyes bright, heads erect, ears pricked back, harness fittings sparkling. The driver, a fine-looking man, sitting straight and firm . . . Down the road they came, in perfect order, the clean bright coach with its shining green body and yellow wheels striped with black, bowling along almost noiselessly behind them. . .

"Now the passengers. Three on the box, four on the next seat and four up on the deck or top seat, six inside with three children, while on the tray two young fellows settle themselves comfortably. Last of all a Chinese goldminer, wearing a new narrow-rimmed boater hat with a black-and-yellow band, and a green patch over his right eye, with many happy grins makes himself quite at home on the hamper."

The tamarillo (Cyphomanda crassifolia), formerly called tree-tomato, is South American by origin and its egg-shaped dark-red fruits have become extremely popular since the 1930s. Strongly flavoured and highly nutritious, they make an excellent cooked desert, add piquancy to pickles and chutneys, and, as in this recipe, make a very interesting addendum to suitable meat dishes.

6 pork chops
2 apples, peeled and sliced
6 tamarillos, peeled and sliced
2 small onions, peeled and chopped
4 dessertspoons brown sugar
4 dessertspoons water

Cook fruit and onion in the sugar and water until just soft.
Trim some fat from the chops, lay in shallow baking tin, pour over stewed mixture,
Bake uncovered in 325°F/160°C oven for about 2 hours.

Coaching: A rest for the horses

Road and air transport

MEAT PASTE OR POTTED MEAT

The elderly aeroplane poking a tentative nose out of the garage door is one of the Bristol Fighters presented to New Zealand by the British Government after World War I. Its biplane wings are stacked on the truck nearby.

New Zealanders were quick to get airborne. Pioneer Richard Pearse has already been mentioned; his first flight was in March 1903, and before World War I began in 1914 a dozen or so aircraft, homemade or imported, had flown with varying degrees of success. During the war two private flying schools trained pilots for the Royal Flying Corps, and 292 of these pupils had won their wings by the end of 1918.

Charles Kingsford Smith was the first to cross the Tasman, in a tri-motored Fokker monoplane, in 1928, and internal air services were well away in the 1930s; but regular overseas services had to wait until World War II had ended.

The garage is advertising two forgotten American cars, Westcott and Dixie Flyer. In the 1920s the motorist had two or three dozen different makes to choose from. The USA had the lion's share of the market, European competition having faded during the war years. And, apart from that, American cars were better suited for rough roads and unbridged creeks, the Ford Model T in particular (at right of photograph) being virtually a cross-country vehicle.

450 (1 lb) shin beef
120 g (4 oz) butter
½ teaspoon mace
½ teaspoon nutmeg
½ teaspoon black pepper, ground
1 dessertspoon anchovy sauce

Put all ingredients into basin with lid and simmer in saucepan of water for 2½–3 hours until meat is tender. Then put the meat through mincer and then add the stock from the basin, mix well and pot.

Lamb or mutton can be used if fat is removed and some chopped garlic used to flavour; or mixed meats with some bacon make a change.

Digging for shellfish

TOHEROA SOUP

Toheroa soup is served in some hotels and restaurants, but toheroas are seldom on sale in the shops. A palatable substitute for the soup can be made from mussels by following the recipe opposite.

The beach in the photograph is typical toheroa country but the children are more likely to be digging for pipis (Paphies australe), a kind of small clam or cockle, much smaller and more abundant than toheroa, and very good eating in their own right.

The toheroa (Amphidesma ventricosum) is a clam up to fifteen centimetres in length that lives in the sand of beaches backed by extensive sand dunes. Maori and Pakeha alike esteem it as a great delicacy, ranking it with whitebait as New Zealand's choicest food.

The toheroa beaches are not numerous and legislation limits the number that may be taken. A fair amount of piracy goes on, but offenders if caught face severe fines.

18 toheroas
1 medium onion
570 ml (1 pint) water
570 ml (1 pint) milk
2 tablespoons plain flour
1 tablespoon butter
pinch of salt
shake of white pepper

To prepare toheroas, wash under running water, and with sharp knife sever each side of the hinge, pull open, remove toheroa but not fringe or suckers.
Wash to remove traces of sand.
Mince with onion.
Place in saucepan with pinch of salt and the water, simmer for 30 minutes.
Strain through fine sieve, pushing all the pulp through with wooden spoon.
Return to saucepan with the milk and season with pepper to taste. Simmer for 5 minutes, remove from heat, add butter and flour mixed to a smooth paste, whisk briskly and then put back and bring slowly to the boil, stirring all the time.
Sprinkle with chopped parsley just before serving.

GROCERIES

This store is suburban. A country store would carry the same range of goods but much enlarged by cooking utensils, textiles, working clothing and footwear, and farmer's requirements such as tools, fencing-wire, rabbit-traps, dips and drenches.

People who remember the old stores say, "And they used to smell so nice!" And so they did. Counter-service was slow but friendly, and the storekeeper and his wife knew more about what they were selling than the supermarket's staff know today.

SELF RAISING FLOUR
900 g (2 lbs) flour
60 g (2 oz) cream of tartar
30 g (1 oz) carbonate of soda

Sieve all ingredients together.

SCOURING POWDER
450 g (1 lb) whiting
450 g (1 lb) soap powder
450 g (1 lb) soap, grated

Mix all together thoroughly, sprinkle small quantity on the article to be cleaned.
Keep in tin away from damp.

BEESWAX POLISH
Grate some beeswax into a preserving jar, then add the same amount of turpentine and linseed oil. Place jar in a saucepan of boiling water and heat until they all amalgamate.
Apply warm for best results.

BAKING POWDER
60 g (2 oz) rice flour
60 g (2 oz) bicarbonate of soda
60 g (2 oz) tartaric acid

Pass ingredients through a fine sieve, keep in airtight bottle or tin.

Grocery, Christchurch circa *1916*

PUKEKO PIE

The pukeko (Porphyrio porphyrio) or swamp-hen is a showy sort of bird, vivid indigo blue in plumage with bright red legs and beak with a frivolous tuft of white feathers at the tail. They are numerous in swampy areas and are regarded as something of a pest by farmers whose crops and vegetable gardens they may raid, and by duckshooters because the pukeko is also appreciative of wild-duck eggs.

They are not considered a great table delicacy, but the pioneer settlers found them an agreeable change from the eternal mutton, and the following recipe is good, particularly if young birds are used.

2 pukekos
2 slices of bacon, chopped
2 large onions chopped
60 g (2 oz) butter
4 medium carrots, sliced
290 ml (½ pint) red wine
1 dessertspoon tomato puree
1 bayleaf
several drops of Tabasco sauce
sprig of thyme and parsley
short or puff pastry

Skin and joint pukekos (young birds if possible), soak 24 hours in salt and water in the fridge. Drain and dry.
Heat the butter in a heavy pan and brown the joints. Remove and keep warm.
Fry onions and bacon until golden, then add carrots, tomato puree, herbs, salt, pepper and the Tabasco sauce.
Replace pukeko joints, cover with red wine and cook gently until tender adding a little water if necessary.
Thicken gravy with a little flour and water if liked.
Line an ovenware dish with pastry, add meat mixture and cover with pastry.
Bake about 20 minutes at 400°F/200°C until pastry is done.

Shooting party

Pink-and-White Terraces

BATH SALTS

The Pink-and-White Terraces of the Tarawera district were New Zealand's premier tourist attraction and were spoken of as one of the wonders of the nineteenth-century world. Judging by old paintings of them they were certainly remarkably beautiful.

But in 1886 the supposedly extinct volcano Mt Tarawera erupted. Three Maori villages were destroyed, 153 persons lost their lives, the landscape was completely altered, and the famous Terraces were obliterated for ever.

A few days before the eruption a tourist party with two Maori guides was crossing Lake Tarawera in two canoes to visit the Terraces. All those in the canoes agreed that they were accompanied at a short distance by another vessel, a Maori war canoe being paddled by one row of occupants while another row was standing, heads bowed and plumed for death with the feathers of the huia and white heron.

In fact there was no such canoe on or anywhere near the lake at that time, and it could only have been an hallucination—or, a phantom seen in broad daylight. The apparition was sworn to by a number of observers of unquestionable integrity. The Maori guides, with good reason, in the light of what was to happen, insisted that the vision foreboded some great disaster. The Pakehas firmly believed they had seen a real canoe.

The Terraces were formed over many centuries by a geyser uphill from the scene depicted here. Its waters, flowing downhill in a fanlike formation, deposited the pink, white and turquoise salts to form a natural feature that sent tourists into ecstasies.

450 g (1 lb) borax
450 g (1 lb) carbonate of soda
450 g (1 lb) washing soda, crushed
240 g (½ lb) epsom salts
some oil of lavender or other perfume

Mix all together and bottle tightly.

OTHER REED COOKBOOKS

THE COMPLEAT BEEFEATER by Lynette Wenham
As well as containing a large variety of recipes for the cooking of beef and veal, this book provides information about the main cuts and tips about selection for quality and economy, storage and preparation. It is an essential compendium of beef and veal cookery for every kitchen.

THE GALLEY COOKBOOK by Gwen Skinner
On the assumption that only limited galley equipment, food storage space and supplies of freshwater are at hand, the author discusses necessary stores, 104 simple recipes, entertaining aboard, food for upset tummies and cooking in rough conditions. Also included are five useful appendices.

THE GOURMET POTATO by Anne Souter
Here are 150 international recipes, including soups, desserts and drinks, catering for every taste: potato and banana pancakes for breakfast, Yugoslavian potato croquettes, or just plain baked potatoes ordinaire to go with anything, any time! Potatoes are not fattening — if you keep you head. This staple food can indeed be made very interesting, and this book shows you how.

BABY GOURMET COOKBOOK by Mary Bayley Fisk
With its extensive range of easy recipes, this laminated, superbly illustrated book is a wonderful gift for new mothers who want to provide baby with food that is healthy, nutritious — and tasty. It warns against dull, over-processed foods and stresses programmes for the introduction of more fibrous dishes.

TRIPLE TESTED RECIPES by Thelma Christie
From carrot soup to steam pudding, potato salad to fruit meringue, and golden chicken to pumpkin pie . . . every cook can rely on this book! Truly tested at least three times, the recipes are wide ranging and interesting.

MAORI FOOD AND COOKERY by David Fuller
Over a period of twenty years, the author has studied Maori hunting, cultivation and culinary practices. This book, the result, contains nearly 100 traditional recipes. It discusses pre-European Maori nutrition, and the creation of a palatable diet from limited food resources.